MY LITTLE ANCESTOR - SO THIS IS GOODBYE

A COLLECTION OF BULLSHIT

M BOU

To my little ancestor,

Khiubam Chawang

For the favor I owe her.

I don't like owing people favors and I don't like them owing me crap!

Let this end the string of fate between us!

I wish you the best!

Happy Birthday!!!

Contents

Contents

Contents

Contents

Preface

My grandma and I didn't always see eye to eye when she was alive. But as an old aged character that she was, she taught me few things about life before she left.

In the family, one was not supposed to casually talk about 'love' if one doesn't mean it. If one doesn't have the courage to see through the ups and downs life throw at us together, that wasn't love to her but just attraction.

Hell, I've liked plenty of women over the years and loved just a number I could count on my two fingers. And most of the time, it still don't work out.

Life is not easy and all you can do is hold your head up high and stick through it.

Let the world burn, but always keep your peace intact. Do not let the naysayers, the haters and the worthless people measure your worth by their obsession to gossip about your life. Do not retaliate and waste your time fighting about stories that are not true. People worth it will believe in you, people not worthy of you would still believe in those web of lies even after you explain it to them.

On that final day, if it ever came and if we ever meet them in Hell, we will roast them together and instruct the Devil which part of them to roast better. Even if we go to Heaven and they to Hell, do not fret, we will just take some days off and visit Hell just to torture them.

Good luck

Acknowledgements

I am not a kind person and I have never learn much on how to thank people.

It does not mean that I am a person who is ungrateful but the people I wanted to thank have mostly left this world. So, I would not be naming names here but just remind my people wherever they are that I remember them, and that it would be better if they can stop visiting me at night when I am trying to sleep.

To the alive, do not try to die so soon. I'll gift you this book to keep you company if you have anything to do with the making of this collection of bullshit.

Thank you.

The Broken And The Damn Tells The Best Stories

"The loudest minds live the loneliest lives"

1. Extraordinaire

My parents
wanted me
to be an
extra-ordinary
man,
while
all my life
I have tried
to settle with
just being
ordinary.
Now
everybody
wanted to be
extraordinary
like it mattered.
Nobody
no longer
wanted
to be ordinary
like
it didn't matter.
I have lost

so many
friends
who leapt
from a
building
aiming
for the sun
and
the moon in
the unending sky,
without
realizing
only
the cold
hard ground
would
welcome them
once
they fall.
If being
extraordinary
meant
such things,
I would rather be an idiot.

2. Chasing clouds

I was a fool
running after your clout,
all the while
knowing how stupid I have been.

3. Religion & Whiskey

As I sat
on my chair
with
my laptop
on my lap,
I began
to think
about
how religion
has killed
the child in me.
My innocence
battered
as I took
a sip
of whiskey,
raw and neat
thanking
the gods
above
for not
limiting

mankind
with the
knowledge of
crafting
alcohol.

4. Women & circles

I liked
a girl
but
all
she wanted
was
to run around
in circles
with me.
Sometime hot
and
sometimes cold.
Maybe
this is why
I have
never
won
an argument
with
the opposite sex.
I should
probably
try my luck

with
the remaining
genders!

5. The Squirter

I took
a girl home
one night
when I was drunk.
I knew of her;
I have
seen her
in the streets
now and then.
But
I don't know
how
she came
into my bed
that night.
I was a drunk
not a gangster.
I just
needed
someone
to play with
for the night,
I was not

looking
for anything
serious
but maybe
just some
30 minutes of serious.
That's how long
I think I last.
I kissed her;
she didn't say much.
She was
as docile
as a kitten
but
bit me
like a bitch
when I
undressed her.
She said coyly,
'no'
and protested
so I replied seriously,
'okay'.
Then I started
fingering her,
that's when
she started

humming
like
a canary
and
rocked her body
to the rhythm
of
my fingers.
Maybe
she sang
too many
heartfelt
songs
the previous night,
when I came
to be
the next day,
I saw
only the juice
she left
on my bed.
That unruly, ill mannered fuck!

6. Love is a word

I did
love you,
maybe
I still do
and
I probably
would
till the end.
But
it doesn't
mean
I won't fall
in love
with another.
Love
is just a word,
hearts
can be transplanted,
feelings
can change.
Nobody
is waiting
for me

at that
end
of the tunnel
and
I ain't
waiting for nobody.
Once
our fate meets
and
the strings
are cut,
that is
when
I leave,
that is
when
it ends.
I'd still wish
you don't get hit
by the next bus
on your
way home
though!

7. To kill without killing

Why do we war amongst ourselves?
I have
seen more
lesser person
kill himself
with
just a bottle
and
a box of cigarette.
As simple as that!

8. To kill an alcoholic

I have
a friend
who lives
on whiskey
as fishes
on water.
I have been
feeding him
with
what I thought
was poison
but the poor bastard
has not been dying.
It has been 5 years now.
What a tough liver
and kidney the bastard has!

9. A bitch and God

Why do we ask for rain
and complain
when God sends a storm.
Kind as He is,
blessing us with a bargain,
more than what we had asked,
and a bitch that you are,
all you know is how to bark.

10. The righteous poor idiots

The poor idiots
who wake
up at 4 a.m
to go to church
and talk
about God,
Jesus
and the Holy Spirit
day in,
day out,
all the while
stealing
a handful
of chicken
from his neighbour
for his lunch
on his way home
from church.
Is stealing considered a sin now?
Or no?
Well,
most had decided

to throw this sin,
punishment,
hell
and Bible ideology
when
it benefits them
most!
These poor idiots,
living on
fantasies
and ideologies,
the kind
you get
only in your
dreams.
They should
be skinned alive
and
let their
greedy souls
run around naked.
Unable to scare people,
unable to get
what they want.
What a terrible life
such righteous people must live!

11. Do not phone a man at 5AM

There are
some stupid,
idiotic people
who think
phoning me
at 5 a.m
would be fun,
when I am
at most
desperately hungover.
Then
they questioned me
on why I didn't
pick their calls
or why
I didn't
call them back
if I saw
the miss calls.
The stupid fucks.
Like
I would love

to hang
with such
ill-mannered
crazy ass
morons
who don't
respect
me enough
to phone me
and
disturb me
when I should
still be
drunk
as fuck.
Well
this includes
mornings,
dusk,
early mornings,
late mornings,
mornings,
early afternoon,
afternoon,
late afternoons,
early evening,
evening,

dawn,
night,
midnight and
whatever time
it is
I have missed
to mention here.
The dumb fucks and their guts.

12. The drunk & the warrioress

Once,
when I was still
a dumb fuck
and
as broke
as a camel toe,
I lived
in a single room
with just
a floor to sleep,
a corner to crap
and
a floor
full of music
once evening
sets in
till
the next morning.
Most nights
I would
be drunk
and would

have passed out.
Those nights
were quite
peaceful,
but
once
in a while
when those
Jesus blessed
sweet whiskey
couldn't
knock me out
as I drink,
I would have
to lay awake
and curse
at the couple
staying
on the floor
above me.
They argue
about
almost everything.
But oh,
the warrioress!
How gallant she was!
I still get

nightmares
some nights
to this day.
Even when
beaten
she would not
stay beaten,
she would clamp
and
crawl her way
back up
to hit
her boyfriend back.
It was
what could have been
a round of boxing
between
Mike Tyson and Bruce Lee.
The guy was
sturdy,
fast and strong
while the girl
was agile
and super-fast.
Their fights were
almost mostly about topics on
'I did'

'You didn't'
'I was'
'You weren't'
'I would'
'You wouldn't'
'I could'
'You couldn't'
'I wont'
'You will'
And such crap. I think.
Well probably
but
I could not
hear them well
as they stayed
on the floor
above me,
so they could
have been fighting
about some
serious topics.
Like the guy cheated on him.
Probably the girl did too.
Anyway,
the only lesson
I picked
up from their fights

was to learn
how to
drink less
and pass out
more often.

13. A jerk & a whore

A group of friends
and I
decided to
gather
and pass our
night drinking,
cursing
at each other.
One insensible retard
brought
a lady friend
to the party
thus
creating
a rift in the atmosphere.
We were probably
too drunk
to notice her,
but
kept our manners
to the end.
We fed her
more whiskey

than her poor stomach
could digest.
She passed out
in the corner.
We kept drinking
and talked about
politics,
economy,
law,
religion
and
whatever topic
we could find,
but some friends
went to bed
the poor senseless bitch
in the corner.
That poor girl
could close her legs
like her life
depended on it.
Well,
her life probably
depended on it
that night.
One was busy
trying

to stick
his oar in
while the other was
busy
pinching her legs
together
like a crab.
After a while,
one guy
successfully
pulled
her underwear down
and hell
it was wet
as an ocean.
I guess
the level
of the foreplay
was probably
professional.
And maybe
the cool wind
hitting her pussy
clear her drunkenness,
she opened
her eyes,
stared at him

and
started screaming
at the top of her lungs.
She was still drunk
but I guess
she knew
about his ill-intentions.
It took 6 of us
to calm her down
and help her
wear her
water-soaked underwear.
The night passed
quietly
till hangovers
woke us up
one after the other.
We ran out of alcohol
to quieten
the voice
screaming in our heads,
our throats were
as dry
and sharp
as our wallets
that were empty.
So we rang

few friends up
telling them
to come for breakfast
with alcohol.
Few of them
came with
a bottle or two each.
We drank
till late at night.
By the time
the sun had set
the lady friend
had fucked
at least 4 of my guys
and she was
all smiles
as she could
not wait
to open her legs.
What a horrible fate!
They should not
have fed her
that plenty of alcohol
and made her drunk
the previous night
if they had
wanted to sleep

with her.
What a slut she was
when she was sober.
I was fine with
whatever they wanted
to do.
The problem
I had with
was with the alcohol
we have wasted on her
the previous night!

14. Some stupid sayings

Some stupid worthless sayings;
'Early bird gets the worm'
is just being selfish,
'birds of the same feather flocks together'
is prejudice,
'health is wealth'
is just plain stupid,
to kill two birds with one stone'
depends on how hard you throw the stone,
'you can't judge a book by its cover'
but what if you have written the whole damn book?
'Perfection'
is just a plain idea bore out of peer pressure
'Seeking attention'
is just a cry for help
'see eye to eye'
is a dumbass saying
when you can only
look eye to eye
when you stare
at another person's eye
or through
a mirror.

It just means
someone is getting
the better end of the deal,
maybe now or
maybe
in the coming days!

15. Debunking the myth of Orgasm & God

Finding God
is like
finding the G-spot
in women.
Only the ones
who know how to,
knows the pleasure
of prayer and orgasm!
For the rest
it's just a myth!

16. Folks with passion

Some folks
are just out there
to hurt you,
they say
the kindest words
and kill you
when you
least expect it
with a smile
on their face.
Some say
the most
loving words
just to keep you
on their hooks
of ego and pride.
Such person
have graduated
with distinction
from
man management
and you should
look

before you make
your bed.
You could end up
lying
on the same bed
without knowing
as they
drain your blood
slowly and painlessly!

17. The Pretenders

They can pretend
all they want,
if you had started
pretending
earlier to their pretends,
what wrong could it do you?

18. Rock & Roll

You can throw
rocks at people
and
roll on the floor.
Just do not
complain
when some dirt get on you!

19. The benefits of twerking

You can dance
and twerk your ass
all you want,
but if it
can't bring
yourself
and your partner
to the promised land
when you finally
jump on his dick.
I say, 'what is the freaking point?'
Everybody can also
do all sort of
useless crap too!

20. Broke with passion

The Old Testament God
was a prideful,
egotistical maniac.
The New Testament God
was a poor son of bitch
who sent
his poor bastard of a son
to be crucified
just to prove
his point.
And some idiots
spend their entire lives
and savings
trying to
decipher
what the gods
above
are thinking.
If that's what
all they did,
I am fine with it
but the concern
was with

how
they wanted us
simple folks
to be condemned
with them
together.
Most importantly,
they have faith
but not
enough money
so they begged
and throw out
any and
every reasons
they could find
in the Bible
to prove their point
and twist them into
earning few bucks
from the rest of the world.
Motherfuckers
should learn
to get the hell up
and earn their own money
to fund their own obsession!

21. Funny thing about fate

Fate brought us together,
destiny interfered.
Life won't let us remain together.
I've learned my lessons now.
I picked my grudges,
licked my wounds and
packed my bag of stories.
I am on my way to
wherever haven
will sheltered me
from the storm that is coming.

22. A disconnect

We live
in a world
rounded with such
advanced
modern
technologies
where
we can connect
with someone
millions of miles
away from home
in a second,
by just a click of a button.
But there is
a certain disconnect
among the humans.
Maybe the machines
have
better rapport
than us.
How is this
not a concern
for someone

with a mind
and a heart?

23. The schemes of gods

I have
never been fond
of the concept
of love
because
it's mostly
about trust
rather than
love itself.
Sometimes
it is based
on circumstances,
and the other
on how
the rest of the world
thinks of you
and your partner.
If you ask me,
it's just a ploy
adopted
by whatever
gods
or demons

above
in their
infinite wisdom
to keep the humans
get so busy
with themselves
that they won't
question whatever the shit
it is they do.

24. The girl with a broken heart

This one
is for the one
whose soul
I had broken
I knew
she trusted me then
But circumstances
happened
And changed
the way
I was portrayed
If entrusted,
I would go back
Not to change
what had happened
But
to love her
better
She was
the reminiscence
of my youth
A better version

of myself
This one
goes out
to the girl
whose heart
I have hurled
Against her own world,
She could
have been just sixteen
full of life and vigor
Even if
for just a short time
But I broke her so,
Still I loved her
And I would be happy
just seeing her smile
and not lose hope
as she go against
the world
for her piece of heaven.
I pray whatever good things
in life there is,
they'd look out for her
As I wish her only the best things in life!

25. They don't deserve it

Let them
remember you
for who
you were
And not
what
you've become
They don't deserve it!

26. The innocence of a schoolboy

We do
the craziest
of shit
when we
are emotionally
wrecked
I had
a fire
burning
inside me
That mooted
out
for lack
of warmth
I can
feel it
rising
somedays
But most
I just
tucked it
behind,

beneath
the charms
of a school boy
Giving hope
to all
Leaving himself none!

27. Farewell from another realm

By the time
she leaves,
I wont be here.
By the time
she reaches,
I wont be there.
She is
just a lil girl
to her momma
Who strives
for better things,
Unafraid
to fight
for what
she thinks is right
She has
big dreams
and huge ambitions,
She would
conquer all
she sets
her sights on.

I just hope
she doesn't
get hurt,
I pray,
hope finds her
before trouble does.
The foes
and the hoes
I pray
they only make her
stronger.
I am not sure
about this ship
we sailing
I lost
the rudder
a while back,
But I pray
she walks out
of this
Alive and wiser,
For all our
bad days,
I hope our
good memories
Keeps the smile
on you always,

Never give up
on yourself
even when
the world does.
Always stay strong
and be happy,
This ain't
a goodbye
but just a
see you
When I see you
kinda fare thee well!

28. Pretty girls and life

I can't seem
to stand
those pretty girls
who know
they are pretty,
Maybe life has not
knocked them
down as often as I would
have liked.
Maybe their hearts
are not as broken as I would
have liked.
Maybe life has a different story for them!

29. Do overs & Start overs

There are
some records
I want to
erase,
Some chapters
I want to
start over,
But
life ain't
about
do overs.
Life is
about
endless
possibilities,
And
in one of
those
possibilities
you'd see me
raise my
middle finger

at you
as I screamed
'fuck you'
and
'fuck the world!'
If life
has been
full of
endless dreams
and start overs,
I would
have dreamt
of plenty more
new ways
to kill
your poor sorry ass!

30. Regrets & wishes in a jar

Some nights
I would
think of you,
Some days,
my mind
would wander
to you.
At all times,
I pray
you would be fine
Against
this brazen
tide of time,
Against
this lazy wave
of crazy minds.
I pray
you would be
alright,
I pray
they would
treat you right.

You were
my youth
personified,
I fell
in Love again,
rightly so
this time round.
Sadly
among all
my sad failures
You were,
my only regret
I decided
to let go of.
I would not
have kept you
Against
this tide of time,
I thought
you deserved
better,
But
sometimes,
I do think of you
And miss you,
thinking about
our what

could have beens,
I hope
you are fine!
Here's to nothing,
but
to all
the fights
And the crazy ride,
I hope you have
plenty more
with the rest of the world.
Thank you!

31. Gratitude

Thank you,
to the foes
who broke me
And
to the hoes,
who cuckolded me.
To the lovers
who
traumatized me,
To the friends
who
blocked me,
To the people
who
abandoned me,
And to my family
who taught me,
I am
what I am
today
Because
of all the pain
You put me through!

32. Another demon

I am not
afraid of
your criticisms
I am
just scared
of my demons
laughing at me
in the middle
of my
sleepless nights!
I am not
fighting
for your
approval
I am
just battling
to survive
against
my insecurities
I am not
living
for your amusement
I am trying

to not disappoint
the people
who stuck around
I am not crying
for your love
I just want
to stop you
from turning
into one of my demons!

33. The Sun don't set in the East

I am
but just a poor boy
from a State
that has taught me
all about failures,
regrets,
scorn,
pain
and a little about success.
Even when the world
calls her names,
even when they pointed
fingers at her,
when people burn stakes
and pour oil
to fan the flames within,
she learnt how to
silently work
for the type of land
she envisioned,
for what her land should be.
She learnt to walk

without a sigh
or a complain
and provide to her people
a safe haven.
Perhaps,
a land still with
unrests and controversies
but a land nonetheless
and nobody
is taking her away
from her people.
The evil,
the corrupt,
the mockery,
the name calling,
the shitty treatment,
the silent judgement,
and what you done to her,
she is over it.
One day, she will
rid of all those things
and more.
If my State can bear
such 'moneypoor',
'corruption',
'a land of evil',
and whatever

other comments people
had given her,
but still dreamt
of making herself better,
who am I to fare worse than her?
Remember,
the sun don't set in the east;
Remember this moment,
when you come
seeking
for some
little bit
of sunshine
from the East!

34. Measure your friends with

I measure friendship
by the amount of alcohol
you treat me with,
when you are nothing
but broke.

35. Drinking to be sane

True,
it is a pity
but I have killed.
I have stolen
plenty of things too,
well who has not?
I have learnt
to ruin good things too
whenever it came,
like a normal human
I have had
my piece of heaven and hell.
But each day,
with the strength
of my own hands
I have pushed
myself up
from the bed I laid,
opened my fridge
with the same hands,
opened
the scotch I had hidden
and poured

myself a drink
to keep me sane.

36. So they say

They say,
'when life gives you lemons, make a lemonade',
but I say,
'when life gives you lemons, find a basket made of stones, wrap them up nicely and throw them back at the person who gave you lemons.'
If you are not
okay with the skin
you are wearing,
if you
wanted to make
something good
happen out of nothing,
without
the failures
and the pain,
how will you learn
to not make
the same mistakes
you made?
It is not
such a good thing
to fit in

with the rest of the world.
Someone
will always
be better than you.
When the crowd
gets too large
and people look
for something unique,
how will you fare
with the rest of the world?
Have faith
in your own path.
Do not
just blindly
follow the crowd.
Be comfortable
with who you are
Be fine
with whatever skin
you wear
each morning
But always
strive to be better
than you were yesterday
Forget the world.
Heaven
will call for you

when they are ready.

Hell

will leave you be

until you are ready.

Focus on your own self!

37. Wishes do come true

MK
had a friend
with whom
he stayed with
for number of years,
and he had really
grown tired of listening to him
talked about his lover
year in, year out.
One night,
his friend went out
and never returned.
The next day.
they found him
face down
on the concrete floor
of his lover's
with his brains blown out.
I guess,
miracles do happen
and wishes do get granted.

38. Rainbows and sunshines

Not everything is about rainbows and sunshines. Not every pasture on the other side is green and lively. Sometimes you got to learn how to dance in the rain.

39. What remembering can do us

As we wilt away
in the silence of the night,
some in pain,
some in trouble,
some drunk,
some high,
some stoned,
some lifeless,
while most of us
trying to get a peaceful sleep,
we remember.
Remember
that the sun will soon be up
and maybe it will be our time soon.
Just maybe!

40. Quitting

I have
a habit of
taking my drinks raw,
maybe that's why
I always have
bad hangovers
in the morning.
I have
maybe twice in a week
always swore
I would
quit drinking.
Now
I am trying
to quit
quitting drinking
and maybe
just drink
as many as I can
and keep puking my insides out.
Comparing
getting nightmares when sober
or having hangovers in the morning,

I'd rather
much prefer the later
and still keep
my sanity
when it's done.

41. The hero that died

My uncle
taught me about
most things in life.
The man
he was then
knew about
so many things.
I would listen
to him like a crazy fan.
I now
so many times
in my own ways
try to
emulate him
but I never could.
He was
an alcoholic
and passed on early.
When everyone
in the family told him
to quit his addiction,
he instead went
to a store

and bought a sunglass
with the darkest shade
he could find,
just so
he could hide
his yellowed
jaundiced eyes.
He later
went out with a bang
and with a drink in his hands.
The same man,
taught me
how to be unapologetic,
to be creative in giving zero fucks,
to not give a damn except for family,
to speak my mind like a man,
to be brave
and to never give up doing what I love.
Since young,
thinking back now,
maybe I had lacked
father figures
and he was
well programmed
and delivered
for me to be one.
He taught me

to write my feelings raw,
unfiltered and unashamed.
The first one.
He was one hell of a man.
He had
his own demons
accompanying him
when the world turn
its back on him.
He had his own wars
to fight but atleast
he never gave up.
You should have met him atleast once.
Then you could have understood us better.

42. Careful of the company you keep

Be careful
of the company
you keep,
Be careful
of the stories
you share.
The same company
once you are away
could sell
your stories
to the company
he wants to keep!
There is no such thing as
lifelong friends
or enemies!

43. The blame game

Who do we blame
for all the shit
in the world now?
If we are blaming God,
I wouldn't want
to be him right about now
If this is hell,
I don't want
to be here when it all blows over
But what if
one day,
we wake up sane
and find the one
running the whole
damn show
is some
homeless guy
acting like God?
Killing and blowing
things up
just because
he is hungry,
mad and delusional?

You pray,
you gossip,
you blame
and you pray again.
What is the fucking point
in doing those
if you are not going
to do anything else?
Take your Bible,
sing Hallelujah
and walk straight
to the depths of hell
when you die,
thinking God
is sending you there
to convince and
make the Devil
believe in Him again?
Remember,
most humans would
fuck you up when you are naked
The Devil
fucks you over
when you are fully cloth,
With bad ideas
and sick propositions
about making

all bad things
go away.
What a poor sod!

44. Maturity has nothing to do with age

Age
doesn't define us,
growing up
does not either.
Maturity
is what makes us
old or young.
We could still
be a child at 60
or a grown up
at 16.
Most of my peeps
mature faster
than the rest.
Sometimes
I wonder
if they would die
quicker
than the rest.
Well,
most of them
are gone now

on their own
preferred ways.
At such
a young age,
responsibilities
piled up
on our shoulders,
at such
an age
we were expected
to mature quicker.
The work,
the pressure,
the headache
eats us alive
each day
but
we go on
about
our way
hoping
these little sacrifices
would unladen
the weight of
the boulders
on the shoulders
of our people!

To the rest
of the world,
we look stupid,
poor and ugly
but
like the thorns
that beautify
a rose,
our demons
make us stronger
and beautiful!
Only
in the dark
could we see
the stars
in the sky,
only
in the dark
would we
be able to
shine the brightest!

45. To the dead and the living

We do not
always
hang out
or talk about
our problems
each day,
but we know
that we would
cross oceans
and build bridges
to come
to help
when needed!
This silent
understanding
enables us
to go out
in the world
brave and ready,
to weather
whatever storms
come our way!

To the alive,
I am always
grateful for
being there
for me
in this
rollercoaster
of a ride.
To the dead,
I remember you
from
time to time
and I hope
the smiles
never leave you
wherever
you may be!
To the rest of the world,
always stay
positive
and be brave!
This world is for us
for the taking
and I pray we stay strong till kingdom come!

46. Angels and Demons

You see
even
the Devil
has wings
so why
do you think
angels
won't have horns too,
it is not
the appearance
that defines them
but their
character.
Just their actions
alone
do not
make them
good or bad,
for
there will
always be
two sides
to the same coin.

What God
considers
a side to be evil
and bad
might be
to the understanding
of the Devil
the only good thing
that could have
come out
of a situation.
What is considered bad
to one
could be
considered good
to the other.
It depends on how you look at it.
It depends on
which side
your trust
will lean with or against.
It depends on how
you interpret a situation!

47. Voices in my head

Finally,
after all the bottles of whiskey
I have emptied and
cigarettes I've lit,
I've found
the demons
I've been
searching for
They were all in my mirror
I've got the monsters
haunting me each night too
They were all in my head!

48. Wet dream & you

Loving someone
like you
is like a wet dream
You feel good
and great
until you come
And ruin everything
The feelings
you accumulate
The excitement
you feel
Only felt real
in your dreams!

49. Success

If success
is your
only keyword
You might
get to the top
But you will
be all alone
Broken, lonely and forsaken!

50. What is and could never be

To all
the friends
I have lost
To all
the people
I may have hurt
To my folks
my peeps
my babes
It was never
intentional
For all
the pain
I may have
caused
I apologise
I was
never right
to begin with,
I was just
out of my mind
Not knowing

what to do
If I ever
lose you.
Then I did.
I am not trying
to backtrack,
Nor am i trying
to shift
the blame.
That was never
my intention.
My intentions
are pure
And I am trying
to find a cure
To all
these bad habits.
I am just trying
to walk out
of this alive,
I bet
on my life
Let karma
hit me twice
Or even thrice,
I won't give a damn!
For all the things

I have done to you,
I deserve it all.
So let me
apologise,
Allow me
to say my grace
In the only way
I know how to,
For better
or for worse
I am trying
to change,
I'll treat you better
next time round!

51. Stone cold killer

She is a stone cold killer
So I learnt
how to
become an ice cold believer

52. Fall gracefully

I am not
afraid
to walk
this road
alone,
I am just
afraid
to be
alone,
When I go
down
This slippery slope.

53. Like the rest of the world

Most of us
Just talked
about it
We dont
go on
and on
about it
We walk on
Alone and broken
like the rest
of the world!

54. The evil of seeing ghosts

I was not born
with a muzzle
in my mouth
You can
call me
by whatever
names
you would like
You won't
see me
blabbering
on and about
many things
in life
But if there is
something
in life
I detest
more than
the schemes
of the Devil
It is those

unloyal twats
who dream
of conquering
the world
by stepping
on the pains
of the rest of the world.
Fuck you
and
Fuck your mama too!

55. God & I

Have I
ever walked
with the Lord?
Probably not
Have I ever
been righteous?
Highly unlikely
Will I burn in hell?
Highly very likely
Do I even care?
Hopefully not

56. How the sun rises in my family

The sun's quiet,
her counterpart's awake
Little soldiers
running amok on riot
With a heartbreak,
scampering on rage
The General's down
on a makeshift bed
Engaged
in a gut-wrenching combat
Lasting long
as for
thrice a season
'Tis the hardest battle
for a reason
But
in the morrow
of the aftermath
The tent screamed
and reeled
with screeching sound
of the squeaky bird

The news
of the birth
of the songbird
Travelled
as quick
as the ray of sunlight
The plight
of the bright red delight
Took a flight
on this white sight,
For the whole camp
since twilight
Had prayed
and cheered for them
For the world
to open
and embrace them.
Now comes
the feast
with the Priest
For the beast
is to be
unleashed,
The battle is won
but not the war
He prepares
for the final showdown

That's bound
to happen
on the horizon,
At least this is
how life is leased,
And how the sun rises in the east!
This is how
the sun rises in my family,
This is how
the sun lights up valiantly
This is how
the sun ignites my vanity,
This is how
the sun rises in my family!

57. A hero & a villain

To be
a hero
you just
have to be
better
at surviving
than
the rest of the world
To be
a villain
you just
have to be
badder
at surviving
than
the rest of the world
And my dear,
one day
that will make
all the difference
in the world!

58. Writing someone off

Everybody
has a story,
a meaning
to their
wretched scars,
Respect
the pain,
Embrace
the man,
Subjugate
the hatred,
We are
who we are
not because
of how
we want it to be
But sometimes,
because
of how
we fell prey
to the trust
we gave somebody.
So

do not judge
Do not curse
And
do not write me off
just yet!

59. A prayer for the departed soul

Of His
infinite wisdom
and Power,
Of a boy
who became
a man,
Of a soul
that never
really left
for home,
Of a body
that left
but
remains
in the hearts
of Hundreds,
if not
thousands,
We bow
our heads
down
in Prayer

And
continue
our work,
all the while
Praying,
'Till we meet again!'

60. Weep not

Weep not
for the
Friend
that is lost
along the way,
Weep not
for the Love
that never
came,
Weep not
for the Pain
that stayed,
Weep not
for the Past
that's written,
Weep not
for the Future
that is not
unveiled,
Weep not
for
the roads
untraveled;

But live
your Present,
today,
without fear!

61. Farewell, my dear

So
this is where
we part,
and tie
Our hearts
in the cart
to find a Home!
This is
not a Goodbye,
but a 'See you Soon';
Not a cry
to the sky,
but a shout to the moon,
Quoted
with devoted lines
from the mind
Of a
doted ally,
to carry you
through the East Wind.
Here,
I pray
you stay fit

till you're gay
and grey,
To betray
the array
of trouble
till you hit
the hay;
Stay immune
to the sand dunes,
yet
be attuned
to the platoon
Of boon
and festoon
awaiting
the coming noon.
To be
the silent
and bright
ray of hope,
not the rope;
To cope
with their sorrow
and mop
their faults!
But still,
with all

being said
and done,
Down the tunnel
when you need
a shoulder,
In good times
and the bad,
the smooth
and the rough
You know
I'll always be
the first one
with you
On the sideline,
smiling
and firing
beguiling queues
Of the same
sarcastic
deliberations
I left you with!
Until that day,
I pray
you take care
And bear
the same health
I am leaving you with!

Farewell,
and Godspeed!

62. To the moon and back

No callithumpians
nor gadflies
can deter me
From going
to the moon
and back for you!
Likewise
the same couldn't
deter me
if I want to stick
the barrel
of a gun
down your throat
and blow
your brains out
if I want to.

63. Let your child

Let
your child
dream a million dream.
Let
your child
aspire and
learn
how to soar
with wings,
to fall
hopelessly
in love,
To make
new friends,
to live NOW
And to believe
in themselves
and not
just in miracles.
Grant them
the chance
to follow
their dreams.

Do not
psychologically
break their minds
Before
they could test
their true
strengths.
A child
cannot be born
with a tag
Like
manufactured goods
to be
shipped;
Teach them
the value
of believing
in a
cause,
Without
compelling
your child
to fulfill
all your
failed ambitions
and passions.
Hammering

more
Nails at
a closed coffin
will only
keep it shut.
Rotten ideas
should not
be recycled
each generation,
You are
in your twilight
Pass the torch on;
Let them
ignite it
with the cause
they
believe in.
If you are
born with shackles
don't mean
Your child
should also
be rid
of sunshine.
Teach your child
about success
and failures,

About loyalty,
hard work,
discipline
and dedication,
But without
exemplifying
or taking cues from
the life of
another's child
It could
all be
just rambles
and shambles.
No child
should be robbed
of who
they want
to be
'Cause of the failures
of another's child,
Every child
is unique,
trust in your own.
Unique talents
should be realized
and appreciated,
You can't tell

a bird to swim,
or a fish to fly
If
they want
to be
admirable
or
educated.
Every child
should be
brought up
uniquely,
A rebellious child
might mean
an unsuitable
Dogma
of upbringing.
That's why
they prescribed
Two children
for a family,
one
for each parent.
Education
should start
from home
into infinity

and beyond.
Long
as you breathe,
you remain
a student.
Many Keats,
Elvis,
Pele,
Adele
remained lost
And unnoticed
in the selfish
dreams
of their parents.
Trust
in your child
to do it right by you,
With bad
experience
we grow wiser,
With good
experience
we become stronger.
Without mistakes,
trials and troubles
We won't be
where we are,

as Humans.
Show them life
as it is,
in Black and White
Let them
color it
with their dreams
and Ambitions.
The future
you build them
would
accompany you
To your grave,
the future
they build
for themselves
Would test
the toughest
of time
and still
stand tall.
Teach them,
guide them
and let your child
leave their own
footprints
behind,

in the sands of time.

64. The moon & the sky

Even if I detest
the vast unending sky,
how could I
ever hate
the moon!

65. A lady & her Prince Charming

You could act
all lady-like,
with
the right make up
and
the right clothes,
The big boobs,
the slim waist,
the juicy fat ass
and
the tight pussy,
no one really
gives a fuck
when
it should matter.
On the other side,
there will
always
be someone
with greater
asset than yours.
So come out

of your little
bubbly
princess world,
you ain't a kid
no more.
learn
how to fight
for
what you want
and not wait
for your
Prince Charming
to come.
The Devil,
you know,
Lucifer,
was once
a Prince
and maybe
he still is,
and man
was he
a Charmer.
The Prince Charming
that
people often
talked about

and for whom
most plain
stupid maidens
wait for,
thinking
they would be
saved
once he comes,
might come
in the form
of the Devil
himself.
A man
with a smile
on his face,
one who is
good with words,
one who you
cannot resist
and one
who will suck
your soul dry
with just
a piece of candy!
Oh, the irony!
So,
be a bitch

once in a while.
Drink if you must.
Flirt if you can.
But do not
become
the Devil
you are
running from.
Learn
how to say
unpleasant
words like
'fuck you'
when situations
demand it.
Be a kid,
be a freak,
be weird,
be all sorts of thing
but only
to the right people.
Perhaps
one day,
you will learn
how to
treat the right
from

the wrong people
in your life.
But hey,
what do I know?
I am
just a drunk
with a bad hangover
who could not sleep
and who had
nothing better
to do at 3 in the morning!

66. The Lamb & the Lion

Inside every lamb,
there is a lion.
Feed the lion
inside you
for a stronger lamb.

67. Love is a phase of time

It is just
a phase of time,
love
is a mood
but so is
pain
and misery.
Like sea waves
hitting
the shore,
feelings
turn into
rhythm
and beat
against
your heart,
so making you
alive!
You can like
a person
but never
love them,
you can love them

but never get
to see
yourself
ending up
with them.
You can love
the right person
at the wrong time,
so can you
love
the wrong person
at the
right time.
There is
nothing wrong
with it.
It is not
a waste of time.
This is how
you decide
your fate.
To either die
in the hands
of a bitch
with a gun
in her hand
or die

like so many
drunks
in the world!

68. My kind of people

I have
made
many friends
along
the way,
I have lost
plenty
of them too.
To those
who stuck
around
knowing
my temper,
my mood swings
and my weird ass
phase in life,
thank you.
To those
who came
to check up
on me
when they
haven't heard

from me
in a while,
when
I didn't reply
to their
calls or texts.
Maybe
I just wanted
to be found
but
wanted
to act
like
a spoiled brat
sometimes.
I know
it is hard
but
let it
be known
that
I really do
appreciate you
for
your patience.
To those
who came

with bottles
of different
flavors
of whiskeys,
I couldn't be
more proud
of you.
To the one
who'd always
get drunk
and
fall asleep
on the same floor
he sits,
to the one
who
would argue
with
some poor
son of bitch
going live
on Facebook
or Instagram
thinking
he could get
his drunk ass
points

across.
And to the one
who would fly
across towns
just to
surprise me
because
one was
feeling down.
Thank you.
Y'all make my life interesting.

69. The losers & the weirdos

Here's to my kind of people.
The losers,
the dummies,
the misfits
and the crazy ass
motherfuckers.
We are the failures,
the fools,
the douches
and lessons
most parents
never fail
to exemplify
when teaching their children.
People looked down on us
categorized us,
called us
the sluts,
the whores,
the dicks
and the assholes,
just because

we won't walk
within the lines
they have drawn for us
But we find
strength
in their disrespect
as the world provides for us.
Gave us
enough reasons
to try
to be better
each morning.
Here's to my people,
who are tagged the weird ones,
the ordinary ones,
the troublemakers
and the rejects
because
we are crazy enough
to be different.
To get up and fight
not for the world
or for what is right
but for ourselves,
to not care
about what they think of us
but to do better,

for we might fail
but atleast
we have tried,
we still try,
try to make
ourselves better
and we never gave up.
So here's to you folks,
I am rooting
for you
as always!
I hope good days
come accompany
you soon after
this storm!
I pray, the gods leave you be!

70. My little ancestor, so this is goodbye

So my little ancestor,
from strangers
to friends,
to the name callings,
to the many things
we have become
over the years,
and to the plenty
of things we could not
have been,
I guess,
life has been fulfilling!
I hope,
you had been happy.
I pray,
I had not made you cry!
I guess,
This is the end
of the ride
for me.
I guess,
this is where

I disembark,
This is where
we choose
different paths.
Maybe,
years down the line
we'll sit down
together
and talked about it,
and maybe
laugh about it,
till then
I wish you the best.
My little ancestor,
So this is goodbye!

71. Like two ends of a rainbow

We are,
but just two souls
connected like
two ends of a rainbow,
the beginning and the end
never to be together
but still connected,
differentiated by its beauty,
united by its complexity
and all it took
was just a spark of sunshine
and a little rain!

Reminiscing About How It All Started

Back when I was just starting out.

When life had fewer problems with me. When I've just discovered the world of the drunks and the stoned.

I went out with a crazy ass lady who was full of wicked ideas. She was fine as a human and friend, but terrible as a lover. She did her best though, I ain't complaining.

It was a crazy ass time.

Friends were aplenty. Most of them have not died then.

We were still young, and the concept of death had not fully slipped across our minds yet. We thought it will all be alright as we grew older.

But maybe because we flirted with death so many times, it has its own consequences.Soon. friends left after another, relations were broken, hearts were ripped apart.

Maybe it was that fragile.

Some got married, had few kids and decided to off himself. Some had few failed relationships and decided to jump from the roof of a building. Some always felt unheard and had problems with their family so they took a rope to end all hopes of living. While some was killed by diseases and in the hands of the gods above.

But some remained and we built a broken home out of it. To this day, only a number of people I could count on my hands remained.

Those crazy ass bastards left for some pastures green. I wish them the best of luck though, and I pray if there is a heaven, they would be let in. They say, 'the good die young', but I call bullshit on it. I have lost so many people over the years, I have become numb to the pain. Complaining about it won't bring the dead back, but I am rambling on about it because I feel for those people out there who had felt the same thing I did, or is feeling the same thing I am now. Like there is no escape, like the walls are closing in and the anxiety which we have subdued wants to fight to be let out. I feel the anxiety attacks, the panic attacks and most of the time I would lock the world out with depression. There is a certain feeling of guilt when you feel happy and when the sun is out, thinking of the people who left because I could have done so much more for them but couldn't and they still left, thinking nobody was there for them. So, I learnt to tune it all out and live with the guilt. You can't hurt what you can't see and what isn't there.

It was all fine and good no matter how many brothers left back then and no matter how many new friends we made along the way only to be lost in time.

My problem with the world back then was because that crazy ass lady of mine left too, without a word, not long after, leaving behind a letter through a friend, with just four words scribbled on it. No tears, no words, no explanation. Just four freaking words!

I guess, this is my story!

A Prayer Before The Curtain Closes

If you have come thus far,
leave my stories where they belong,
but pick the pieces in your heart
and I pray you continue on
with your story.
Before this crazy world
eats you alive
and leave you with nothing but trouble!
Protect your peace at all costs
and never lose your sanity.
Innocence is overrated!

Love & Time

When love turns into obsession, it's time to let go!

The End

This marks the end of my career as a writer, author, poet and songwriter.

Thank you for sticking around.

I wish you all the best!

9 798887 830315

Printed by Libri Plureos GmbH in Hamburg,
Germany